10 THINGS

Great Coaches Know

A Leader's Guide to Athletes, Team and a Winning Culture

By Gary Pritchard and Mike Tully

Disclaimer – Any improper or missing credits for the stories
and quotes contained in this book were unintentional.
The authors deeply regret any errors or omissions.

Dedication

To my wife Patty and daughters Leigh Ann,
Tricia and Katie.

To my friend and mentor, Dr. Rob Gilbert.

To my friend and mentor, Dr. Carl McGown.

Mike Tully

Thanks to Christian Arendt for the cover and book design.

To all the great coaches who shared their thoughts with us
and to my mentor Dr. Rob Gilbert.

Special love and thanks to *my team* Todd, Scott, Sean
and wonderful wife Kate.

Gary Pritchard

Contents

Introduction

Once upon a time a group of penguins looked up at some birds soaring overhead and they began to wonder, "How come they fly and we don't? We all have wings." So the penguins hired a consultant and attended an all-day seminar. At first it didn't go well. Every time a penguin hopped off the special flight training platform, he crashed. For the entire morning session, there were more bruises than flights.

After lunch, the consultant's expert training began to take hold. With growing confidence the penguins embarked on progressively longer flights. Near the end of the afternoon, they were quite a spectacle. They soared, swooped, dive-bombed and did everything the other birds did.

Finally, their session ended and the consultant received not only a standing ovation but a flying ovation as well. All were overjoyed at the growth and accomplishment. The consultant saluted the penguins for their progress as they headed out the door. And then the most amazing thing happened...they all walked home. Many people are like those penguins. They get great information, then never use it.

10 Things Great Coaches Know grew from the many discussions between Coach Pritchard and Coach Tully. This book reflects a deep passion for coaching. Our hope is every coach who takes the time to read this book will use it as a resource, discover some new tools, and get a fresh perspective on things they already know.

Great coaching is truly an art. It must be studied, practiced, refined and valued for its hard-learned lessons. In this book, you see a great appreciation for the many hats you must wear: teacher, leader, motivator, tactician, technician, planner and more. We wish you all the best in your endeavors and journeys as a coach. May we never take for granted the opportunity we have to touch peoples' lives and make a difference.

CHAPTER ONE

It's Not About You

*"The best way to forget one's self is to look
at the world with attention and love."*

RED AUERBACH
Hall of Fame basketball coach

"A lot of people have gone further than they thought they could because someone else thought they could."

UNKNOWN

Here is a story about a young man named John.

He played a couple of seasons on Coach Tully's co-ed volleyball team when he was in seventh and eighth grade. He was neither the best nor the worst player on the team, just a young man who walked into our gym and was welcome there. Coach Tully recalls:

A couple of years ago, while walking into a farmer's market near our home, I heard a voice.

"Coach Tully! Coach Tully!"

I had no idea who this young man was until he introduced himself as the one who played on my team years earlier.

He was now attending college, and earned money in the summer by managing the farmer's market. It was so good to see him, and it felt good to have a former player greet me so warmly. Now and then I would see him at the market and we always talked.

Then came devastating news just before Christmas. John died tragically.

His obituary contained the following words:

He loved volleyball.

He loved volleyball!!

What a humbling feeling to read those words. In our gym, he had found something he loved. That's the thing about coaching. You can give athletes something to love, something that will make a difference in their lives. And your influence can reach all the way to a player's obituary.

And that is the first thing great coaches know: It's not about you. It's about the athlete. It's about fun and learning and creating good memories. It's about what the athlete can take into life when the game is over.

It's so easy to forget this. Coaches are human, even if parents and fans don't always think so. And being human, coaches sometimes focus on the wrong thing. They think about their win-loss record, the banners on their wall, and even awards and their place in history.

Don't get us wrong! We love coaches who win games, especially when they do it with exemplary values. We look up to them, follow their seasons, and look to them for insights. We quote many of them in this book. But coaching is not about wins, or banners, or about you as a coach. It's about the athletes. Players have a value that goes far beyond whether or not you win today's game.

At the Montclair Kimberley Academy in Montclair, New Jersey, headmaster Tom Nammack meets with the coaches early every year. And every year he emphasizes two points.

1. The time an athlete spends with you might be the best part of his or her day.

2. Players aren't mind-readers. If they're taken out of a game, tell them why.

Don't let them sit and guess.

With each of these points, Nammack was reminding his coaches that it's about the athletes.

Years ago, Coach Tully shared gym space with a wonderful theater director named Kathy Thomas. After school, the volleyball or basketball teams would practice. Then they would move out and Kathy would bring in the singers and dancers for play practice.

It was during those times when Kathy Thomas taught a secret of theater directors. At a certain point in the rehearsal process, the director starts moving farther and farther from the stage. Each day brings just a little bit more distance between the director and the performers. This is the director's way of letting go and letting the performers fly on their own. With this distance the director is acknowledging that the performance ultimately belongs to those on stage.

Then when the applause comes, it goes to the performers, not the director. That's the way it should be in a game. When the team wins, credit goes to the athletes. Win or lose, the coach must think about how the experience can help the athletes grow.

Coaching should be the same way. Coach Pritchard often speaks of empowering the athletes rather than directing them. By the time athletes leave your team, they should know a little bit more about how to pursue success, how to make decisions. Coach Pritchard loves the saying, "Life's a bowl of choices."

Sometimes a coach's greatest moment can come when he does nothing. Arsene Wenger, manager for Arsenal FC in England, once said, "Sometimes the hardest thing as a coach is to do nothing. But if you keep faith in your players, it often comes right. It is good for athletes to work through challenges and build resolve."

Coach Pritchard emphasizes that a good coach is a questioning coach. He will ask athletes questions, for instance: "What do you want to accomplish this season?" "How do you want to improve as a player?" Then the coach designs activities meant to help the athletes meet their goals. Along the way, the coach can keeping asking, "Are you doing what needs to be done for you to accomplish what you said you want to accomplish?"

Through this process, the coach teaches accountability. It's the player's dream, the player's actions, and the player's results. What greater service could a coach provide for athletes than to point out the connection between what they DO (effort) and what they GET (results)?

When Coach Tully was playing freshman baseball in high school, the coach brought him in to bail the starting pitcher out of a jam. He forgets the details, but remembers doing well and going to the bench after the inning.

A man in the stands said to the coach, "That's quite a lefty you have there." To this the coach replied, "Yeah, but wait until next inning." In other words, don't expect too much from him. He can't sustain it.

Years later, an athlete will remember an exchange like that one. With those few words, the coach made a player feel less valuable. He could have said something inspirational. But he didn't. To be clear, Coach Tully was never going to reach the big leagues. The coach's words didn't make a difference in that respect. And his words didn't leave scars that required lifelong therapy. But he had a chance to motivate and inspire. He didn't.

Every time you speak to your players, remember that lesson. Just a few words either way can make such a difference. This doesn't mean you must pamper your players. Just the opposite. You show respect for them by challenging them. Some coaches can criticize players and fill them with confidence. Other coaches, unfortunately, can leave their players feeling deflated no matter what they say.

One of the biggest thrills you can get is hearing one of your players say that something he or she heard in your practice helped in another area of life. Just a few weeks before this book was published, one of Coach Tully's juniors passed her driving test. Afterwards, she was kind enough to say that the breathing exercises she learned came in handy in the nervous minutes before the test.

By empowering a player you are preparing him/her for life.

Through coaching, you can make players comfortable with risk. Look at American football, and how many passes you see thrown in a game. Teams pass, even though when they put the ball in the air, three things can happen and two of them are bad:

One, a teammate can catch the ball (that's good).

Two, no one catches the ball (that's bad).

Three, an opponent catches the ball (that's really bad).

So why do teams throw passes when so many bad things can happen? They do it because not passing would make them so predictable that the other team would always win. In other words, the risk of passing is essential to success.

Success and failure aren't opposites. They are more like the "hero and the sidekick." So you must encourage your athletes to take chances, to expand their comfort zones, to experience and manage risk. It's about them.

A good coach will try to learn what makes each player tick, what motivates him/her, whether he/she is an auditory, visual or tactile learner, how to speak to each player, and what his/her interests are.

Taking the time to learn these things shows that you care. In the end, it comes down to the expression, "No one cares how much you know, unless they know how much you care."

In the book *The Talent Code*, author Daniel Coyle offers this question about coaching:

"Are you a 'sage' on a stage or a 'guide' on the side?"

It's not about you!

Notes:

What about this chapter did you find most interesting?

What point will you put into your next practice?

Be honest. How much of your coaching is about the athletes?

What attitude change would most affect your decisions?

CHAPTER TWO

It Really *IS* About You

*"You get the best out of others when you
give the best of yourself."*
HARVEY S. FIRESTONE
American industrialist

"Leadership is a matter of having people look at you and gain confidence, seeing how you react. If you're in control, they're in control."

PAT RILEY
Championship NBA coach

Coach Tully recalls:

Years ago, I helped supervise the baseball desk at United Press International.

Every April we hired three summer interns (we called them dictationists) to help with the massive workload. An ideal intern could take dictation from various ballparks around the country, re-write copy, edit stories and work in a demanding environment, all while bringing a knowledge of baseball.

It was a tough assignment, but the survivors went on to prestigious positions elsewhere in the news business.

After a few years, I noticed a pattern. Every single season, one of the interns would be outstanding, one would be mediocre, and the third would be poor. Even back then, long before my coaching career began, I wondered something. Perhaps the quality of the dictationists had less to do with them than with me. Was it possible that they were responding to my expectations?

Today I am sure that was the case. I made decisions on their ability early in the game, and most of the trust and work and responsibility would go to the one whom I judged to be the most talented.

So without fail, much of the summer experience became a reflection of what I thought of the summer staffers. In other words, the team was all about me.

It's the same way with coaching. Teams take on the personality and habits of the leader. Everything about you says something to the players. Very impressionable, they constantly look at the coach and form their own opinions: Jose Mourinho, manager of Inter Milan Football Club in Italy, once said, "Coaches are role models for players and fans. They have a duty to behave better than anyone else." Do you think, look, act and speak like a coach? Are you professional? Compared to all these questions, the issues of strategy and knowledge and drills finish a distant second.

As the authors of *Freakonomics* put it in their chapter on parenting, "It isn't so much what you do as a parent, it's what you are."

Players will look carefully at the coach to see how he/she responds to every situation. Everything from the way the coach handles adversity, to his/her level of focus, to his/her character, goes on display. And none of it will escape the team's notice. If players see a difference between what a coach says and what a coach does, chances of team success dwindle quickly.

Coach Pritchard heard a wonderful story that illustrates what a coach means to the team's personality. We're not sure of the source, and apologize to anyone not receiving credit.

Once there was a hard-working father who, with the best of intentions to do well at his job to provide for his family, kept breaking promises to play with his son. One night, the boy interrupted his father's work and asked to play with him for just a few minutes.

To keep his son occupied, the man grabbed the newspaper and turned pages until he came upon a large, detailed picture of the world. He tore out the page and cut the picture into small pieces, saying, "If you can put this back together in 30 minutes I will play with you. I promise."

Thinking he had occupied the boy for a while, the father was surprised within minutes by a tap on the shoulder. "All done,

Daddy," the boy said. Not believing the boy, the father went to the dining room table and saw the completed picture.

"How did you do that so fast?" he asked.

"Daddy," the boy replied, "As I was putting the globe together I noticed on the back side there were pieces of a large man. "I started putting the man together. Once I had the man right, the world was right."

And so it goes with coaching. If the man/woman is right, then the world is right. If the coach has character, sets goals, shows compassion, exhibits fairness, the team will likely follow.

If the coach walks the walk, players will, too. But if the coach lectures on fitness while munching on a doughnut, the players will notice. If the coach demands detail while showing up to practice without a plan, no one should expect the players to take all the lectures seriously.

Good coaches must demand great things of themselves before they can ask for great things in others. Legendary football coach Vince Lombardi attended church every day. Baseball manager Tony LaRussa spends his road trips holed up in his hotel, looking for any detail that can help him win a game. Hockey coach Fred Shero studied the Russian hockey program back in the day when copying the Soviet Union was not the popular thing to do. By blending Russian skating with Canadian toughness, Shero won two Stanley Cup championships. None of it would have been possible without his research.

Coaches create the team personality with their style. For example, there's the best management technique in the world: Catch someone doing something right. What a difference when someone is recognized for good things, instead of being criticized for something bad.

In Coach Tully's gym they play a game designed to show that your attitudes shape the way you see the world. First he asks the athletes to take a look around the room and notice how many articles are red. He tells the athletes they are in a competition. When the minute is up, he starts the competition by asking everyone to name all the BROWN articles in the room. Naturally the athletes protest that the game is unfair. That's when you tell them the moral of the story: You tend to see what you are looking for. If you look for red, you will tend to see red. If you look for the bad in others, you will surely see it. If you look for the good, then the good will emerge, too.

For coaches, it's easy to see which players are too slow, too small, too this or too that. It takes a special coach to see — and to let players know — what they do well. When coaches value everyone, regardless of talent, skill or position on the team, the players know that and respond. If coaches separate players according to ability, and have special rules for the stars, the team chemistry will suffer. So it's all about you.

Great coaches are acutely aware of how their actions affect the whole. In the New York Yankee dynasty from 1998 to 2000, Joe Torre won three World Series by brilliantly managing the personalities — some of them very high-profile and well-paid — in the clubhouse. Torre was particularly effective at keeping a productive relationship with team owner George Steinbrenner, notorious for firing managers.

Casey Stengel, when he managed the Yankees in the 1950s, said, "On every team there will be five players who love you, five players who hate you, with 15 undecided. My job is to keep the five who hate me away from the 15 who are undecided."

Top coaches provide a consistent atmosphere. Consistency in practice leads to consistency in games. A stable culture, free from extremes, lets players concentrate on building skill. Wild swings of emotion mean that players must use up valuable mental energy trying to figure out which version of the coach has shown up on a particular day. Sarcasm can confuse players. Coaches should say only what they mean.

Consistency must apply to ethics as well. Some coaches deal in situational ethics. A violation that might bring a suspension one day suddenly gets overlooked before a big game. That leaves the players wondering what the rules are and to whom they apply. It also makes the players roll their eyes the next time the coach wants to talk about discipline and values.

Likewise, a coach who complains about the officiating is helping to create a team personality that looks for excuses and scapegoats.

In short, coaching is all about you. It's about the energy, the example and the philosophy you bring to practice every day. If you find yourself consistently seeing a flaw in your team, such as failure in the clutch, an inability to close out games, a lack of focus or a lack of commitment, it's time to take a look at where and how the group developed this personality.

Notes:

What qualities do you believe your players see in you?

If you could change one quality about you, what would it be?

What are you willing to do to make this happen?

Which qualities do you find most inspiring in others?

CHAPTER THREE

Teach Values, Not A Sport

"The values learned on the playing field — how to set goals, endure, take criticism and risks, become team players, use our beliefs, stay healthy and deal with stress — prepare us for life."

DONNA de VARONA
Olympic swimming gold medal winner

"No amount of ability is of the slightest
avail without honor."

ANDREW CARNEGIE
American industrialist

When he first sat down to organize the 2008 United States Olympic basketball team, Coach Mike Krzyzewski asked his players to mention something they felt was important to team success.

One of them said that the players should be on time. Another emphasized that there should be no excuses. Think of that for a moment. Here are some of the best basketball players in the world. They make millions of dollars. Yet when it came time to pursue an Olympic gold medal, they started with basic values: punctuality and accountability.

So it should be in your program. Coaches love the Xs and Os, and the whole process of putting together a team and a strategy. But the basis for greatness always begins with values, and the best coaches let their players know that.

Success in life comes from the same things as success in sports: Hard work, teamwork, honest communication and commitment.

Teaching values reminds Coach Pritchard of those snowball fights he had when he was a kid. Remember this trick? You toss a snowball high in the air. When your opponent's eyes are fixed on the sky, you sneak in another snowball, nice and low, to the chest.

Coaches can do the same in their programs. While the kids have their eyes on the fun, you can sneak in values and life lessons. A great way to do this is through stories. Our mentor, sports psychologist Dr. Rob Gilbert, is an expert storyteller who has taught us how a well-told tale can help make a lesson stick. He and Coach Pritchard wrote a book called *105 Great Stories*.

Some coaches like to be more direct. They put values front and center.

Ollie Gelston, a celebrated basketball coach at Montclair State University in Northern New Jersey, had this rule: "Be in the right place at the right time and do the right thing." That's not just a sports-practice thing, it's a life thing. It can apply to going to work, going to school or fulfilling any responsibility you may have.

Many professional sports coaches have run a team with only two rules: Be on time and work hard. Those rules capture so many values: punctuality, responsibility, accountability, discipline, effort and persistence.

The coach can teach players responsibility through what Coach Pritchard calls "the chain." Values form attitudes, which in turn create choices. Kids make choices, and those choices have consequences. Repeated choices make habits, habits make character, and character makes destiny.

As a coach, you have only a short time to make a real impact on your players. Ten years from now, players won't remember the plays or the score of the games but they will remember the thoughts and values you taught them. Ask yourself, are you teaching short-term for the win, or long-term for the person? Do you develop the whole person? Are you giving your players tactics to win games or tools to help them succeed in life?

You can always be on the lookout for chances to grow. If you let it, the game will teach wonderful lessons. We can learn:

- An appreciation for consistent hard work and effort
- The importance of a great attitude and how you see things
- The choice between getting frustrated or fascinated
- Whether we perceive a problem or a possibility
- If any given situation is an obstacle or an opportunity

- The satisfaction of working with and helping others
- How to work toward a goal
- The value of practice and preparation
- How to deal with pressure and competition

Great coaches explain that sport is like life. It is not always fair. We get bad breaks. We get bad calls. We get bad bounces. Mistakes will happen. And just because we are nice people doesn't mean we will be successful. That's like the vegetarian in a bull ring in Mexico thinking he/she is safe because he/she doesn't eat meat.

Quotes and anecdotes can help the lessons sink in and stick. For example:

"Master the art of temporary failure." This helps young people understand that failure need not be permanent and that it's how you respond to failure that really counts.

"Success leaves clues." One way to achieve success is to follow the example of others who have done so.

"Feedback is the breakfast of champions." Emphasize that there are two kinds of people: Losers and learners. Everyone loses, but not everyone learns from the defeat. Part of that learning is to understand that when coaches offer feedback, it is not criticism but belief in your potential to improve.

"If you don't stretch your limits you will set your limits." In many programs, "can't" is one of the most frequently heard words. No one ever achieved greatness by living in their comfort zone.

"A setback...is a setup...for a comeback." Everyone feels inspired by tales of those who overcome adversity. Each bit of adversity gives you a chance to write a story of your own!

"Great people do their best when they feel like it least." You probably would not like it if you were getting on an airplane and overheard the pilot say, "I'm really not into this today." Same way if you were being wheeled into the operating room and the surgeon told you, "I don't feel like doing this."

"Everyone who got where they are...started where they were." All persons of prominence, whether TV personalities, sports stars or great entrepreneurs, started as unknowns. If that's where you feel you are right now, you are in great company.

Introduce your players to some of the great women and men who lived by the qualities you want your players to exemplify. Basketball legend Bill Russell was the ultimate winner who always put team success ahead of individual statistics. Coach John Wooden spoke of balance and love. Wilma Rudolph overcame childhood polio to become an Olympic champion. Coach Pat Summitt flat-out will tell you, "We will outwork you."

There are so many others: Roger Bannister, Mia Hamm, Michael Jordan, Thomas Edison, Helen Keller, Albert Einstein, Abraham Lincoln, Mother Teresa, Walt Disney, Rosa Parks and Ray Kroc. All of them, in one way or another, exemplified the values of hard work and persistence.

Their example will come in handy on days when your players confront things they can't control, like bad weather, poor field conditions, officials' mistakes, parents, other players, etc. Teach players that while they can't always control their circumstances, they can control "**E-A-R:**" **E**ffort, **A**ttitude and **R**esponse. Again, these are life concepts, not just for sports.

Teach that learning never stops. You are either moving forward or going backward; there is no such thing as standing still. Pick one "life-lesson" word a week for your players to focus on. These are the things you want your players to carry with them.

One week, for instance, the word might be "respect." Coach Summitt has made this the first item in her "Definite Dozen" for creating a program's success. Another week the word might be "character" or "integrity." If you think this is too much for a young athlete to handle, think again. Coach Tully's grandchild — at age four — has a "Word of the Month" in his karate class!

You can, as Coach Krzyzewski did, sit down with your players and ask them for input on values that they think will be important to team success. You will be surprised — and inspired — by the answers.

Finally, in dealing with your players, ask yourself this question, Do you want to be successful or significant?" Teach values.

Notes:

What lessons on values can you take from this chapter?

Which values are most important for any program?

What is your style for conveying values: Stories? Anecdotes?

Something else?

What are your favorite quotes?

CHAPTER FOUR

Motivation Over Evaluation

"You can motivate by fear, and you can motivate by reward. But both those methods are only temporary. The only lasting thing is self-motivation."

HOMER RICE
Coach and college athletic director

"Passion, not pedigree, will win in the end."

JON BON JOVI
American musician

Years ago, a wise man in the press box told Coach Tully that the most interesting day of the baseball season is August 15.

That may surprise you. Occasions like Opening Day, the All-Star Game and the World Series seem much more interesting than August 15.

But that's exactly the point the wise man was making. Anyone can get excited about those special occasions. But not everyone can get excited about August 15. That's the day when most players wake up and feel the mental and physical fatigue. They say to themselves, "Ouch. We've been at this every day for four and a half months, and we have a month and a half to go."

Pro sports seasons are a marathon, not a sprint, and to win you must find motivation somewhere. Day after day, your teammates are counting on you. People are paying to see you play. Aches and pains are no excuse. Where are you going to find the energy to meet that kind of challenge? In their own way, scholastic seasons are as demanding as professional ones. They may not be as long, but they are filled with challenges all their own: teenage angst, academic pressures and time demands, not to mention the emotional ups and downs of the season.

Faced with this landscape, students need inspiration. That's where the coach comes in. Someone has to help the student-athlete through the daily grind of performing at a high level. Otherwise, they walk in a world of constant evaluation, on tests, on SATs, on driving tests, college interviews, or even comparing themselves to others.

Once upon a time Coach Tully knew a New York sports writer who took infinite care with every story. People marveled at his attention to detail and how much of himself he sacrificed to make his story just the way he wanted it. One day someone asked him what motivated him. He said, "Every time I write a story, I imagine that a Broadway star is going to be reading it tomorrow."

Therein lies a powerful lesson for coaches, namely, that motivation is where you find it. You can invent, dream, or research. Anything — as long as it is within ethical bounds — can work as effective motivation. Nothing seems to work as well as a sense of mission. Remember the Knute Rockne story about winning one for the Gipper? He was calling on the players' sense of tradition, something higher than themselves. Then there was Herb Brooks' chilling call to destiny before the United States Olympic hockey team went out to face the Soviet Union in 1980: "You were born to be a player. You were meant to be here."

Both of these legendary speeches took place either before or during a game and were intended to produce focused emotion on one day.

But there's an even more important kind of motivation. It's the kind that calls you to work hard day in and day out. It is nothing less than a call to live a certain way, so that when, for instance, August 15 of baseball season arrives, you can find the motivation within.

Tommy Lasorda led the Los Angeles Dodgers to a pair of World Series titles not because he was a superior tactician but because he was a peerless motivator. He made the Los Angeles Dodgers the most important thing in his professional life and he wanted others to think that way, too. He referred to God as "the Big Dodger in the Sky." Lasorda often said that when cut, he bled Dodger blue. To him, motivation was not a big-game thing. It was an everyday thing.

Same way with the Montreal Canadiens hockey team. In their locker room, a sign proclaims: "To you with failing hands we throw the torch, be it yours to hold it high!" Once again you see the power of calling upon something greater than the player himself/herself.

Lasorda and the Canadiens' tradition both demand that you live, act and think a certain way, in accordance with the highest of standards. And this mental approach is necessary because improvement is hard work, very hard work.

Do you know of the concept called deliberate practice? We will speak about it in detail in Chapter 6, but for now, let's just call deliberate practice the blueprint for excellence in any field. It offers an excellent return for the effort you put in, but it's very demanding, and here's why.

In deliberate practice, the thing you are working on at any given moment must be just outside the area of your competence. Consider what that means. Most people like to work on things they already know. Unfortunately for them, this won't lead to peak performance.

On the other hand, those pursuing greatness are never quite comfortable. They are constantly working on things that don't come easily. Do you know how much motivation it takes to live in a world where you are never quite comfortable? That's where the inspiration comes in. If you want to help someone become great, you must make the vision so powerful that it will help them through all the pain.

For example, the next time you see Olympic figure skating, look past the pretty costumes and the grace. Think of how much discomfort went into the performance. Not only did the athletes have to constantly work on things just beyond their area of competence, but chances are they had to wake up at 4 o'clock in the morning just to experience that kind of pain!

No wonder there is the story of how one Olympic athlete motivated herself to get up so early. On her bed stand she placed a picture of her rival, along with a printed message that said, "While you were asleep, I was practicing."

So if you want your players to get better every day, they will have to feel a little pain every day, and you will have to provide the inspiration to help them get past that.

All this raises the question of whether motivation comes from within or can be applied from without. A good coach recognizes that no matter how inspiring and motivating their techniques may be, it is still external motivation and can lose effect over time. The key is to spark internal motivation in your players. You can ignite desire and persistence and a "want to do it" attitude. If there's even the tiniest ember glowing in someone's belly, it's the coach's job to keep it burning. Renowned sports psychologist Dr. Rob Gilbert says that it's the coach's job to give hope.

Some motivational techniques are brilliant in their simplicity. Bobby Hurley, legendary high school basketball coach at St. Anthony's in Jersey City, New Jersey, makes sure to compliment every player in the first 20 minutes of practice. Not only does the praise make the players feel good, but it prepares them for the tough coaching that is certain to come later in practice.

In Coach Tully's gym, there is a "quote of the day" on the whiteboard, not only to motivate but as a tie-in to the points to be mentioned that day. Occasionally, to get the athletes thinking about motivation and inspiration, Coach Tully will present a quote and challenge them to find a better one.

Not all the motivation is verbal. Research shows that when one person speaks to another, only seven percent of the meaning comes from the actual words that are used. Some 38 percent comes from the tone of your voice, while your body language accounts for 55 percent. That means that even by the way you stand, or sit, you are sending messages that can motivate or de-motivate your team!

Keep these ideas in mind: The best management principle in the world is to catch someone doing something right. And remember to praise in public and correct in private.

To summarize, if you had to rank the top duties of a coach, you would have trouble choosing between teaching and inspiring. Teaching certainly is high on the list, but it works best when the audience is motivated to learn. You can give all the great speeches you want on the day of the big game, but if you haven't inspired your players to do the daily, painful hard work of getting better, then all the pep talks in the world won't matter.

*Dr. Gilbert, offers a daily motivational hotline. It's free. It's called "Success Hotline," and you can call it right now at (973) 743-4690. Coach Pritchard sends out the "Thought of the Day," and Coach Tully produces a blog **www.totalgameplan. com** that is designed to motivate and to teach.*

Notes:

What thoughts on motivation and inspiration can you take from this chapter?

What thoughts or quotes could make an impact with your players?

Will you share these with your athletes?

When? And in what form?

CHAPTER FIVE

Team Culture is Everything

"If there is a mutual respect between players and coaches, that keeps the team honest and makes for a very healthy environment which in turn promotes other important qualities such as work ethic, integrity and a positive atmosphere for competing and winning."

JILLIAN ELLIS
Assistant coach, U.S. women's national soccer team

"I think a lot of our team commitment is a silent understanding that each one of us has poured our life into what we're doing."

CLAIRE CARVER-DIAS
Olympic synchronized swimming bronze medal winner

Back in the 1950s, when the New York Yankees seemed to win the pennant every year, any rookie with sloppy work habits would soon hear from the veteran players.

"You're messing with our wives' fur coats," the veteran players would say.

This was the veterans' way of telling the young players to clean up their act. In those years, before the era of huge salaries, the extra money players got from reaching the World Series really made a difference — the difference between a wife getting a new coat or not. Anything that put that bonus money in danger had to be stopped quickly.

That's when the veteran players stepped in to remind the young ones about the expectations. Anything less than a trip to the World Series was unacceptable, and so the preparation and focus had to be on a championship level. In other words, "That's how we do things around here."

"The way we do things here" is the team culture. Every sports program has one. Some cultures are good, some not. But every team has one. Anything and everything can set the tone, but at the root is the question of standards.

When teams decide on their standards, they are also deciding on their destiny.

This means that teams must be very careful when picking standards. Just because a team believes that it has a healthy culture doesn't necessarily mean that it's true. Sometimes there's a laziness or sloppiness that has seeped in and become accepted. For instance, if enough people wander late into practice without being called out by the coach or their peers, then, no matter what the players say, everyone has reached an agreement that being on time doesn't matter. No matter how much talent and skill is on the team, and no matter what words or slogans the team uses, this effort will be fatally flawed.

In other programs, however, there is a rich culture carefully cultivated by coaches and zealously upheld by the players. These teams understand that you are only as good as your last game or practice, and that talk is cheap. They work hard every day to deepen the culture and the tradition. They really mean it when they say, "That's how things are done here."

This understanding need not involve words. One day, Coach Tully proudly invited world class United States Olympic volleyball coach Carl McGown into his gym. It was soon obvious Coach McGown was not impressed. He was more interested in the clutter in the corners than in the size of the facility. "You can't have a sloppy gym, because you don't want anything sloppy going on in your gym."

A neat gym. That is culture.

Every year, legendary basketball coach John Wooden invested time in teaching his players how to put on their socks. New players would be surprised, and perhaps a little disappointed, to see a great figure like Wooden concerned with such mundane things. But it was anything but mundane to Wooden. He saw a chain: a poorly fitted sock leads to a blister, a blister leads to missed practice time, missed practice time means subpar preparation, and subpar preparation means subpar game performance. Whether it's about expectations, the neatness of your gym, or wearing socks properly, the smallest details can represent a powerful idea: We are committed to doing things right.

Here are just a few ideas you could consider in building your team culture. Note that in each case, there is a meaning that goes beyond the simple physical action.

Team culture starts with a strong base: Dr. Jerry Lynch, author of *The Way of Champions* and *Thinking Body, Dancing Mind*, speaks of building blocks to a strong team culture. All teams are not the same, and you, as a coach, can help guide the members to their particular values and beliefs. Dr. Lynch suggests such core ideas as respect, trust and accountability.

One of Coach Pritchard's foundations in team building is: Knowing your role on the team and, *most importantly*, accepting it.

Coaches like to preach: "Always team above yourself." But does the reality in your program match the preaching? Would your athletes agree that the team is first with you, or would they say you put certain players or situations above the team?

Build a total program: If possible, you should work with the youngest age group to teach them your culture and how things are done at the upper level. Get them inspired at a young age and at a time when you can make a great impact.

Have your players come down and mentor the younger athletes in the program. This will inspire the younger ones and give them role models. Be sure to get the full mileage out of it by inviting the younger ones up to watch their models play. You will enjoy seeing how models play when their students are watching. This will produce instant accountability among your players.

Develop team leaders — groom them early. They will pass down the tradition and standards of your culture while mentoring and setting an example within the team. Empower them to handle some of the responsibility of managing certain team issues.

Develop rituals: Rituals are a huge part of team culture.

Everything matters, from the pre-season routine, to pre-game warm-ups, to practice, and to post-game activities. Even how uniforms and numbers are handed out can be part of the tradition. Hazing, on the other hand, can actually disrupt the culture and can create serious issues and should not be tolerated.

Culture means details. Here are a few suggestions:

- **Always look the coach(es)** (or any person you are addressing) **in the eye.** This not only shows respect for the person with whom you are speaking, but also reflects enough character and self-belief that you are able to look people in the eye.

- **Shake the coach's hand at the end of practice every day.** This is a chance for you as the coach to make one last point or to get a read on what's going on with your players. Legendary high school basketball coach Bobby Hurley says he wants to resolve all conflicts before the players go home for the day.

- **Act like a winner at all times.** Your body language on and off the field/court is paramount. There is no time for moping or feeling sorry for yourself. Players in a pity party are only a distraction to others. It's unfair to have your teammates asking "What's wrong with so-and-so?" when they should be concentrating on improvement. One of Coach Pritchard's remedies for a pity party is to hand the player a Q-Tip. When the player responds with a puzzled look, Coach says, "Quit Taking It Personally. It's not about you. It's about the team and getting better."

- **Give world-champion effort at picking up equipment and helping teammates.** Coaches can learn a lot about players by watching them get ready for practice or picking up afterward. Some players will pick up only what's close to them. Others will actually roam through the gym/field, looking for the stray items that others might have missed. As for helping others, you can gain insights into your athletes by watching how they pair off. In small group practice, you want your better athletes to deliberately choose a weaker player to work with and to help. Most times what you see is the opposite. You see a better player choosing another strong player to have an easy go of it and not look bad to the rest of the team.

- **It's a family.** Create an environment where players feel safe and are encouraged to take risks, as well as to speak up without fear of retribution. There must be a respect for each other's differences, as well as for strengths and weaknesses.

  Remember that your team has a culture. It's either a healthy one or an unhealthy one. It either encourages growth or inhibits it. Your job is to create the right culture, so that what goes on in practice and in the hallways produces greatness on the field/court. Whether it's with words, actions or habits, you want your players to believe they are part of something that is greater than themselves and is first-class.

Notes:

What can you use from this chapter to improve your team culture?

List two concepts you will integrate into your program.

What would your players suggest for details on team culture?

How closely aligned would your details be with theirs?

CHAPTER SIX

Praise Is An Art

"Where there is no difficulty there is no praise."
SAMUEL JOHNSON
English author

"It doesn't take talent to hustle."

H. JACKSON BROWN JR.
American author

Back in his sports writing days, Coach Tully worked with a young woman who used a lot of semicolons in her stories. This is unusual in sports writing. Most of the time, sports stories should be direct. Sentences shouldn't even be long enough to need semicolons.

One day her colleagues asked this young woman why she used so many semicolons in her writing. Her answer should get the attention of any coach. She said, "Because I was once praised for knowing how to use them correctly."

Years later, during one of his college coaching seasons, Coach Tully caught some grief from his players. This was not at all unusual during that season. His team didn't win many games, so there was lots of grief to go around. But like the answer given by the young sports writer, this particular grief should get the attention of any coach. It seems that the players did not like the way Coach Tully gave out praise. They felt he was praising the wrong things.

Those two stories give coaches a powerful message. Praise can make an impression that athletes carry for life, so it should be given in the right way, for the right reasons, and to the right person. Praise can underline your values and serve as motivation, both to those who are receiving the praise and those who are nearby. Trouble is, there are tens of thousands of words in the language, and in any situation the coach must choose the right ones for greatest impact. It brings to mind the story of the young author who wrote to a publisher and asked, "How much do you pay for 50,000 words?" The answer came back, "Which words and in what order?"

It would certainly help to have some guiding principles. Fortunately, there are some. First, praise things that are within the reach of everyone on your team, namely effort, progress and attitude. Second, give the athletes a clear roadmap for how to receive recognition. Develop and make known the behaviors that you value, and then praise them when you see them.

Author Po Bronson goes deep into the subject of praise in a 2007 New York Magazine article called "How Not to Talk to Your Kids: the Inverse Power of Praise." Though aimed at parents, the article could also apply to coaching. It cites research by psychologist Carol S. Dweck that provides a simple formula for praise: focus on effort, not talent.

For a look at effort and talent, recall the tale of the tortoise and the hare. You probably heard the story in grade school. The speedy hare and the plodding tortoise decide to race. The hare sprints far ahead, so far ahead that he decides to take a nap. Meanwhile, the tortoise keeps putting one foot in front of the other. When the hare finally wakes up, he sees that the tortoise has overtaken him and is drawing close to the finish line. Mustering all of his speed, the hare races toward the target. But the tortoise gets there first, winning the race.

After witnessing this athletic event, which would you praise, the hare's talent or the tortoise's effort?

Too many coaches make the mistake of praising the hare. They see an ability that smacks them between the eyes, and they soon find themselves saying something like, "With talent like yours, just imagine what you could accomplish if you worked really hard!"

Great coaches always praise the tortoise. Here's why.

Praising effort is an invitation to everyone on your team. Whether they're big or small, strong or weak, fast or slow, agile or clumsy, your athletes can give full effort, make progress or show great attitude. Praising talent can often exclude some players because they will never be as big, strong, fast, agile or graceful as others. By praising effort, progress and attitude, you clearly show what you value, and players can choose how they will respond.

Effort gives consistency to everything in your program. Effort works in offseason training, it works in practice, and it works in games. Coaches preach that "You play like you practice." That's true, but most teams don't practice with nearly the intensity necessary to excel. If you can establish a program grounded in effort, you will have given your team a glimpse of greatness. On the University of North Carolina's women's soccer team, a culture of competition means that players must either give full effort or fall behind. In the weight room, in sprints, or in drills, North Carolina players understand that their rank on the team depends on their effort. The praise comes in the form of having an improved score posted on the team rankings.

Effort keeps your athletes in the moment, where you want them. Athletes get in trouble when their thoughts wander to the final score. They concentrate on the outcome, not the process, and this is a fatal mistake, because it's the process that determines much of the outcome. If you concentrate on winning or losing (the outcome), you feel stress. If you concentrate on full effort, the outcome is often victory. Competition is full of distractions: the score, the referees, the conditions, and emotional ups and downs. Concentrating on effort simplifies the game.

You transmit a life value when you praise effort. You help create a success formula to carry the athlete through any challenge. Motivation comes in two forms: external and internal. Motivation can occasionally work when it comes from the outside, but it always works when it comes from within. You can praise an athlete all day long, but what happens when you're not there? By calling attention to effort, you tell the athlete what's necessary for continued growth. By praising effort, you help athletes make a connection between what they do and what they get.

It's a cycle: "The harder I work— the better I perform, — the better I perform, the better I feel, the better I feel — the more I like it, the more I like it — the harder I work." And the cycle continues.

On the other hand, praising talent gives players a disincentive to improve. After all, why should a player work if he/she already enjoys the admiration of the coach or parents? The player praised for talent thinks, "They value what I already am." The player praised for effort thinks, "They value what I am becoming."

To fully appreciate praising hard work over talent, it's important to remember a concept mentioned earlier, namely, deliberate practice. This is a very special kind of activity that can yield dramatic increases in skill. Elements of deliberate practice are: a conscious effort to improve, repetitions that are many and measured, accurate and relevant feedback, and activity that is just outside the player's area of competence.

It's this last idea — operating just outside the area of competence — that defines top performers. They are always practicing something that they haven't quite mastered. Think about the situations that make you uncomfortable, such as trying to speak a foreign language, speaking in front of a group, walking into a party where you hardly know anyone, etc. These situations can be awkward almost to the point of being painful.

Yet hard workers care so much about improvement that they are willing to spend hours in that world every day. Don't you want people like that on your team? Don't you think that their willingness to tolerate discomfort might make them tougher in the heat of competition?

This appreciation of hard work can make you a superior talent scout. You will spot prospects where other coaches will not see them. For instance, in the younger age groups, coaches often perceive talent when what they are actually seeing is one youngster who is a few months older than the others. Older and therefore bigger and stronger, this child is a star at a certain age, only to level off a year or so later.

While the other coaches are looking at the man/woman-child, you will be looking carefully at a younger child, a child who does a great job of improving. This young athlete pays attention, looks the coach in the eye, absorbs information and puts the effort behind it. This child can be the tortoise who will soon overtake the hare.

This brings us to the "Sunset Syndrome." Have you ever marveled at the beauty of a sunset? When you're gazing at the spectacle, you don't think of the physics of light. You merely enjoy the show. Coaches are like that when it comes to improvement. They see it, marvel at it, even praise it. But they never give much thought to the underlying causes: why certain players improve more than others do. They never look at improvement in terms of a principle and a backbone of a program.

Dr. Carl McGown has given a lot of thought to the subject of improvement, and he discusses it at his Gold Medal Squared volleyball coaching clinics. He emphasizes this point: Initial ability and final ability are not closely related. The more you coach, the more powerful this idea becomes. And it leads to a question: If initial ability and final ability are not closely related, then what is in the middle?

Here's what's in the middle. The amount of deliberate practice that you are willing to put in. Certain people will give you more effort in practice than others do. They force themselves to engage in demanding, awkward, nearly painful practice. That is why it makes no sense to praise talent; it has very little relation to final ability. Praise effort.

Notes:

What can you use from this chapter to help raise the effort of your athletes?

What impact might this have for next season and in future team selection?

Are there parents in your program who could benefit from learning to praise effort over talent?

How could you approach this?

CHAPTER SEVEN

Measure Progress

"In all human affairs there are efforts and there are results, and the strength of the effort is the measure of the result."

JAMES ALLEN
New Zealand diplomat

*"Face reality as it is, not as it was or
as you wish it to be."*

JACK WELCH
American businessman

On January 16, 1973, in the dead of winter and about midway through their first season in the National Hockey League, the New York Islanders played the Minnesota North Stars and lost 1-0. The game could have gone either way, but it was still a loss for the Islanders. As they left the arena that day, they carried this record with them: Four wins, four ties, and 37 losses. It couldn't have been much fun. And the season still had 11 weeks to go.

Fast-forward several months. A man is sitting in the press box at Nassau Coliseum on Long Island, New York, stopwatch in hand, monitoring an Islanders game. Every time the puck goes into New York's defensive zone, he clicks the stopwatch on. Every time it leaves the zone, he clicks it off.

****

In the last chapter we talked about praising effort, not talent. But here's a question: What exactly is effort? Is it working up a sweat? There are tons of teams that work up a good sweat without putting in any real focused effort. Coaching legend John Wooden warned against confusing activity with accomplishment.

According to the dictionary, effort is the *exertion of physical or mental power*. But this definition isn't enough to describe what happens in an effective practice. Real improvement comes with the *exertion of physical* AND *mental power*. Body and mind must both be involved. Making practice really mean something involves focused DOING and THINKING. To get your athletes physically, mentally and emotionally involved, remember this: If you want to improve performance, measure it. If you want to improve performance more dramatically, then post what you measure. This brings us to the five reasons to measure progress.

- **It's fun.** Did you ever see that look on someone's face when they accomplish something for the first time? Nothing beats it. It feels good to get better. Coach Tully knows of a coach who ties strings of various lengths to the basketball backboard. At key points during the season, she has her players jump to see which of the strings they can touch. As they reach progressively higher strings, they know they have improved their jumping. No one has to tell them, they see it. Another milestone to celebrate.

- **It's motivating.** When athletes see their improvement, they don't just stop and savor it. They want more. Reaching for that string on the basketball court becomes the connection between the hard work and the result. Now, as their coach, you get to validate. "You've been working really hard on your exercise program, and it shows."

- **It gives H.O.P.E.** (Hang On, Possibilities Exist). Sometimes, when your team is in a mismatch, you have to think more about small attainable steps than about winning the competition. This is "the game within a game." Take, for example, a lacrosse team trailing by five goals at halftime. To give this team hope, you can focus on a stat like ground balls. Make it a goal to win more ground balls in the second half than in the first half. By measuring the process (certain things we need to do) versus the outcome (the final score), you can help the players have more fun and improve their focus.

- **It builds confidence.** Once athletes make a connection between what they do and what they get, they have learned a life skill that goes far beyond the sports arena. Once they have seen the progress that comes with focused effort, they can use that effort in the classroom and other aspects of their life. Thomas Carlyle said, "Nothing builds self-esteem and self-confidence like accomplishment." With all these benefits coming from progress, a coach's job becomes clear: Create opportunities for progress, look for signs of it, notice it, praise it and measure it.

An example: A former pro basketball player named Joyce Bukowiec taught Coach Tully an outstanding pre-practice warm-up drill. It involves standing four feet from the basket and shooting until you make four baskets from that spot. When you make four, you can move to another spot and start over. This is a great way to empower athletes to measure their own improvement and strengthen their self belief. *Before practice has even started.*

- **Helps with composure.** When athletes are being measured, they are competing to improve their score. As the intensity increases, so does the pressure. By measuring things in practice, you are helping the players deal with game pressure. The game is not against your opponent. Many times it is against yourself and how you can raise the level of your performance. Players have more composure on game days when they have already faced intensity and pressure in practice.

Exactly what you measure, of course, is crucial. Management consultant Dr. Peter Drucker famously said, "What gets measured gets managed." Or, you can put it this way: What you measure is what you value.

For years the baseball establishment valued the *wrong thing.* When it came to measuring the effectiveness of batters, it computed a player's batting average, that is, the number of hits divided by times at-bat.

Then along came an amateur statistician, Bill James. He argued that batting average was a poor indicator of a batter's value. James's idea was to measure the batters' on-base percentage instead. That is, times on base divided by times at-bat. To James, it didn't matter HOW you got on base, as long as you did. For a while, the baseball establishment resisted this concept and kept measuring the *wrong thing*. Today, thanks to James, on-base percentage is recognized as an important measure of a batter's effectiveness.

Three things are worth mentioning here. First, James did a lot of his early writing while he was working as a night watchman in a pork and beans factory in the Midwest. Second, he had no credentials whatsoever as a baseball expert. He simply had an intense curiosity about the game, and explored this curiosity.

Finally, his work came along at exactly the right time. Baseball salaries had begun to explode, and people on both sides of the contract negotiations desperately needed to answer the question: Exactly how good is this player? How do we measure his performance? And there was Bill James, providing answers that few others could.

Put all these factors together, and it's clear that your measurements need not be fancy, and you need not be an expert. You simply need a deep curiosity about your sport, and a desire to improve your team's performance.

While it took baseball more than a century to measure the right thing, the Islanders — with whom we began this chapter — needed only one year. In analyzing their disastrous first season, they could have found dozens of things to improve, but they boiled it down to one simple thought: They had allowed too many goals.

Of course, poor defense is a common problem in many sports. But not everyone responds the way the Islanders did. They made a commitment to reducing their goals-against by measuring it. Someone once said, "What gets measured, gets done. What gets rewarded, gets done well." The Islanders wanted to do things well.

Remember that man in the press box who was holding a stopwatch, measuring the amount of time the puck was in the Islanders' defensive end? The idea was simple. The more time the puck spends NEAR the net, the greater the chance that it will wind up IN the net. So, suddenly the question about performance becomes much more focused and manageable. It's not just about preventing goals. It's about mini-questions like: Exactly why did the puck spend so much time in the Islanders' end of the ice? Was it a bad pass? A mental error? Poor positioning? Slowness of foot?

Each bit of information can lead to new questions and answers, each time improving quality. If it turns out that the pass was bad, you can ask: Why? Was it poor fundamentals? Carelessness? Perhaps the receiving player was not in a good position? The more you know, the more you have a chance to know.

In their second year, the Islanders lowered their goals-against total. Soon they became an elite team. Within just a few years, they won four consecutive titles. And a simple stopwatch was part of it.

Russ Rose, coach of the powerhouse Penn State women's volleyball team, measures two kinds of statistics: the ones on the traditional score sheet, and his own. The traditional stats measure things that happened. Rose's personal stats measure things that should have happened *but did not*.

Think of how many ways you can use Rose's technique. Let's say you coach a basketball team. You surely measure how many points your players score. And, you measure their percentage of shots made. But do you measure their percentage on shots that are wide-open and within range?

As a soccer coach, do you count how many times your team fails to clear the ball? Or, how many times a player's pass misses a wide-open teammate? These are all things that should have happened but did not.

Any talk of measuring progress must surely lead to a discussion of goal-setting. Without goal-setting, your efforts are like driving your car down the road and not knowing your destination. Goal-setting is a topic unto itself, but one of the basic elements of any goal is to be able to measure progress.

For instance, say you're shooting only 60 percent from the foul line and you'd really like to get that number up to 75 percent. Once you know where you are, and where you want to be, you can decide how to get there. And, you can measure the progress.

Peter Ueberroth, head of the 1984 Los Angeles Olympics and onetime commissioner of baseball, had a favorite saying: "In life you are never standing still. You are either moving forward or sliding backward." Measuring gives you exact knowledge of whether you really are moving forward. It also gives you pride and joy of accomplishment.

Whether it is team performance or individual performance that concerns you, make sure that you measure progress in games and practice alike. It can make all the difference.

Notes:

What do you measure in your program?

After reading this chapter, how confident are you that they're the right things?

What weakness in your team could improve if you measure progress?

Will you do it?

10 Things Great Coaches Know

CHAPTER EIGHT

Find Mentors

*"Better than a thousand days of diligent study
is one day with a great teacher."*
JAPANESE PROVERB

*"The greatest good you can do for another is
not just to share your riches but to
reveal to him his own."*

BENJAMIN DISRAELI
British prime minister

Unless you're a huge sports fan, you've probably never heard of Ralph Jones. Born in central Indiana in 1880, Jones coached football, basketball, perhaps even a little baseball.

He coached for a long time, with better than average results. But his records don't tell you everything about his legacy. At Crawfordsville High School and Wabash College, he coached and became a role model for a young man named Piggy Lambert. Lambert himself became a coach, and he met a young man who loved to play basketball. That young man grew up to become perhaps the greatest coach of all time. His name was John Wooden.

In looking back over his career, Wooden gave credit to Lambert, who, in turn, had noted the effect that Jones had upon him. Who knows what Jones would have said about his influences? One thing is for sure: Coaching can involve wonderful role models. A good coach will seek them out, ask them questions, model them, and then, hopefully, become a mentor to others.

Do you remember this quote? It was the heading for Chapter One: "A lot of people have gone further than they thought they could because someone else thought they could."

If you want to become a great coach, you must find that "someone else" in your life. A mentor will care, teach and motivate. Mentors can guide, advise, open doors and help you with their network. Life is short, too short for you to make all the mistakes by yourself. So learn from the mistakes of others.

As the saying goes, a mentor is the difference between taking the stairs or riding the elevator.

You can have one or more mentors. They can be young or old, in your field or not. A mentor can be a coach, a teacher, a parent, or some expert in a particular field. In baseball, the mentor is most often someone in your own clubhouse. In 1993, sports writer Leonard Koppett published a book called *The Man in the Dugout: Baseball's Top Managers and How They Got That Way.* Koppett identified three managers — Connie Mack, John McGraw and Branch Rickey, all of them born in the 19th century — who still strongly influence the game. All three were part of a chain of coaches that goes back decades and continues indefinitely into the future. In their day, they sat on the bench, rode trains and lounged in the clubhouse, either soaking up knowledge or dispensing it. Today, the men whom they influenced are riding airliners and emailing files of important information.

No matter what the era, this is what great coaches do. They find knowledge. They seek out mentors. But you must choose wisely. In fact, you may be saying, "Who is the right mentor? How do I find him/her?"

It's a great question. Judging by the way some coaches behave — yelling, baiting referees and intimidating players — it's obvious that they have chosen poor role models. As these words are being written, two college football coaches have recently been fired because of abusive treatment of players.

Make your mentor someone whom you respect outside your sport. Choose someone you admire, but don't put anyone on a pedestal. The more time you spend with anyone, the more you realize that he/she, like everyone else, is imperfect. Instead of putting your mentors on a pedestal, put them under a microscope. Study them, because success leaves clues. Here are some pointers on identifying and working with mentors:

- **Look for someone with a strong philosophy.** Coaches who win year after year do so, no doubt, because of deeply held beliefs. These beliefs are easily expressed, though it may take players some time to let them sink in. Pat Summitt, legendary coach of the University of Tennessee's women's basketball team, has even published the beliefs on which she has built her program. They are called "The Definite Dozen," and she explains they are the key to sustained success. Hall of Fame baseball manager Joe McCarthy offered his "Ten Commandments for Success in Baseball." And people listened; Joe DiMaggio once said, "Never a day went by when you didn't learn something from McCarthy." Wooden, in recounting the influence Lambert had on him, referred to Lambert's strong principles. Remember, great coaches hold strong beliefs, and hold to them. Some coaches win now and then because they are fortunate enough to have good players. Long term, nothing replaces a strong belief system.
- **Show genuine curiosity in the subject matter.** Your curiosity will open doors with even the most famous coaches. Everyone has some ego. People enjoy being asked their opinion. It's hard to imagine any coach who, if asked respectfully, wouldn't share knowledge. If your mentor is really worthy of your time and admiration, chances are they have spent a great deal acquiring the expertise that interests you. It will be flattering to them to be asked about something in which they are so fully invested. Take a mentor to lunch. Here are some suggestions on questions to break the ice and keep the information flowing.
  - What are the three most important things you focus on with your team and athletes?
  - What is your philosophy as a coach?
  - If you had the chance to do some things over, what might you do differently?

- What has worked well for you?
- What were the toughest decisions you ever had to make as a coach?
- How do you handle balance between your personal life and your coaching?
- Who was the coach who influenced you the most? Why?
- Who was the most challenging athlete you coached? Why?

These questions show genuine curiosity, and most people will respond well to them. Soon, you may even find yourself invited to watch practices, or even to offer your own opinions.

- **Give back.** After a while, if you truly are passionate about learning in your field, you will discover things that even your mentor does not know. When this happens, share! Dr. Rob Gilbert, a famed sports psychologist who is a mentor to both Coach Pritchard and Coach Tully, always enjoys hearing motivational quotes or any detail about peak performance. It's extra satisfying when you can offer Dr. Gilbert — an expert in his field — something he finds useful.
- **Be yourself!** Don't try to copy your mentor; there's already one of those. You are one of a kind, and you offer a package that no one else can. Learn from mentors and build upon their work, but think for yourself.
- **Be Respectful of your mentor's time.** Everyone is busy. You want to have a definite understanding with your mentor of when, where, and how frequently you meet. Also, establish the best way to communicate between meetings.

You need not work with a mentor directly. In fact, you can receive a lot of great coaching by visiting a library. North Carolina basketball coach Dean Smith, Pat Summitt, baseball manager Joe Torre, and North Carolina women's soccer coach Anson Dorrance have all written books about their success. So have dozens of other coaches and athletes.

Football icon Vince Lombardi is the subject of countless articles and books. There are entire Web pages devoted to his quotes. The wisdom can go back decades and is available to anyone with a computer or library card.

You can own the collective wisdom of history's great figures. Even if you pick up only one little tip from each book, you will be a better coach. Write down every tip or quote important to you. Learn. Who knows? You may find yourself with a great book and, before you know it, you will soon be the authority, and you will be mentoring others!

Ultimately, what do you want from a mentor? All of life is a search for strategies. Our mentor, Dr. Gilbert, has a success equation that goes like this:

$$AB + ST + \text{"GOYA"} = +/\text{-}R$$

This is what the equation means: You have all the ability (**AB**) in the world. Take that ability, and find a strategy (**ST**). Then take action ("**G**et **O**ff **Y**our **A**natomy") and you will get a good or bad result.(**+/- R**).

This equation perfectly sums up the difference between winners and losers. When losers try something and get a bad result, they decide that they don't have enough ability, and they quit. But when winners get a bad result, they decide they need a new strategy.

In other words, your strategies, and not your ability, will determine what you achieve. So a great part of life is the search for winning strategies. That's what you study in your mentor. How does this coach handle an unmotivated player? How does that coach structure practice? What are the mentor's best tips on technical training?

Coach Pritchard believes passionately that success leaves clues, and he is always searching for one tidbit to add to his coaching knowledge.

Even when you're alone in your practice, you can make your

mentors work with and for you. For example, make believe your mentor is with you when you write your next practice plan. Ask yourself these questions:

- Would your mentor be impressed with the level of care that you put in?
- Would your mentor believe that the time spent with you was worthwhile?

When it comes time for practice, you can use the same technique. Pretend that your mentor is there with you or watching from the stands. What would your mentor see? Would there be knowledge, discipline, passion and correct habits and attitudes? Remember what Hall of Fame baseball player Phil Rizzuto said about having DiMaggio as a teammate? He said you never wanted to play bad in front of DiMaggio. *As a player would you have dreamed of playing poorly in front of a coach you respected?*

If you care enough to seek out a mentor, then chances are you are gaining enough knowledge and experience to become a mentor. It's probably already happened for you. You've taken a liking to someone new in the business, and you've begun to help them.

As you yourself become a mentor, notice the qualities that make you want to help someone. Chances are the person will be, as we mentioned above, curious, respectful and eager to give back when given the opportunity.

To find and become a mentor involves the excitement of the unknown. Like Ralph Jones, who was part of a chain that produced John Wooden, you can never fully know what part you might play in this epic. Baseball guru Branch Rickey knew a young pitcher named Tommy Lasorda, but he never lived to see Lasorda become a great manager. Who knows whom Lasorda has already influenced?

But this chain doesn't work all by itself. The search for a

mentor must begin with a great passion, which in turn will lead to great curiosity. Albert Einstein once said, "I am no genius. I am merely very curious." Our wish is that the same passion and curiosity that created your mentor will nurture and develop your talents to mentor others.

Notes:

Do you have a mentor(s)?

If not, write down two or three coaches or people you would like as a mentor.

Will you contact them? All you have to do is ask.

Are you a mentor to others? Give back.

CHAPTER NINE

Keep On Team-Building

"Cooperation is the thorough conviction that nobody gets there unless everybody gets there."

VIRGINIA BURDEN
Author

"Almost all of our limitations are self-imposed. Those that are not can be overcome by cooperation with others whose strengths complement our weakness."

BILL KOCH
American skier

On October 11, 1974, one day before Game 1 of the World Series, John "Blue Moon" Odom and Rollie Fingers of the Oakland A's had a fistfight in the clubhouse.

Every once in a while, you will hear a story like that. Teammates tussle for a while, someone breaks it up, and then the combatants tell the press that the occasional clubhouse blowup is part of the game.

And they're right. Friction on a sports team is natural. There is so much that can go wrong. The season is long, with ups and downs, and filled with jealousies and moods. There are different personalities, and tempers and frustration. No wonder there are some fights now and then.

Trouble is, on most teams, the tension never produces a fight. Instead, the issues simmer, unspoken except behind someone's back. This kind of tension, unlike the sort that exploded in the Oakland A's clubhouse, can wreck a team without the coach even knowing about it.

That's where team-building comes in. Great coaches are always paying attention to the chemistry on their teams. There's never a time when you can say things are perfect. Pittsburgh Steelers Hall of Famer Lynn Swann once described the challenge of getting along by asking this rhetorical question: Can you block for the running back who just stole your girlfriend?

It's impossible to make everyone happy all the time, but team-building exercises can remind everyone about common purpose.

Coach Pritchard specializes in team-building and team dynamics, and can make the experience meaningful and fun. His sessions not only build unity and cohesion, they also help to identify leaders, show which players are most fully invested, and point out potential conflicts.

Team-building requires a delicate balance for a coach. On the one hand, you must be on the lookout for possible problems, and organize ways to build camaraderie. On the other, you can't force things.

"Our job is to facilitate and moderate," according to Coach Pritchard. "It's not up to you to fix everything. The team has to work things out. Your job is to constantly monitor the pulse of the team and ensure things stay on track and functioning in the right direction."

"Allow leaders to emerge to help with the responsibility of managing the team with accountability and discipline. Help the team to have a sense of ownership. It's their team; you're just a part of it. Help players understand and develop their own roles on the team, and most importantly, accept their role for the team."

Team-building activities come in various types:

- **Social**. This includes pasta parties, potluck dinners, barbecues, community service, going to the movies, bowling, dances, ice-skating, etc. Coach Tully's teams have a tradition of lock-ins, where the entire team goes to one player's home and stays overnight. Community service is also a powerful unifier. Besides helping the community, this activity also sends the message that players are called to give more than they receive. Community service can range from cleaning up litter to volunteering at daycare centers to collecting warm clothing for the needy in winter.
- **Physical**. This includes team challenges in running or

various exercises. There can be low-rope and high-rope courses. Coach Pritchard's obstacle courses, in which some players are blindfolded, develop a profound sense of trust. Other activities require complete cooperation from all members to achieve some physical goal. A good book we recommend is Greg Dale's *101 Team Building Activities: Ideas Every Coach Can Use to Enhance Teamwork, Communication and Trust.* You can also find stories about teamwork in the previously noted *105 Great Stories* by Coach Pritchard and Dr. Rob Gilbert.

- **Psychological**. This includes mental and emotional development. Team members learn to let go of mistakes. (How frustrating is it to be trying to win a game when a teammate is having another pity party?) Lessons also include staying in the moment, correcting team focus, understanding game momentum and seeing how team chemistry must adapt with substitutions and injuries.

Pre-season is an excellent time for team-building because it can combine the social, physical and psychological elements. The team is eating together, sweating together, learning together, and struggling together. Coach Tully's teams usually go away for at least one overnight trip during training camp. Riding the bus, eating and socializing brings the team together. Something about the shared experiences of travel makes a deep impression.

Once the season begins, the sessions should continue, though they may change form. After all, there probably won't be as much time for extended sessions as there was in pre-season. In their place, you can incorporate team-builders into warm-ups or cool-downs.

We warn our players about gossip, reminding them that, "Anyone who will gossip TO you will gossip ABOUT you."

Little rituals like "game buddies," in which players decorate each others' school lockers, work wonders. So can team slogans or special team phrases. The Boston Red Sox called themselves "Idiots," helping them remain just loose enough to win the 2004 World Series.

It's also fun for a team to pick a mascot, give it a name, and even invent a personality for it. A bulletin board can remind players about their shared accomplishments and goals. A quote of the day written on the board, especially if everyone on the team is invited to post a good one, also contributes to the sense of team. What's most important is that no one be excluded on the basis of ability or playing status.

Valuable though these daily rituals and symbols may be, organized sessions often become useful — even necessary — at various points of the season. Before big games, after tough losses or any time that team confidence is down are all occasions for team-building. Keep in mind, as mentioned at the start of the chapter, tensions can sometimes slip into team dynamics before the coach knows. It's important you watch for the little things. It may be a look shot at a player, a snicker or a sarcastic comment. Catch these and address them so little problems don't grow into big ones.

Naturally, some people will be more open to team-building than others. For example, an athlete who has an issue with playing time or role might resist team-building or even be contemptuous of it. But in reality, during team-building sessions this athlete has a chance to shine above the starters and earn respect for his/her contribution and ideas. A good coach will seize the coachable moment and explain how every player has value and a certain role that contributes to the team, even if it's not a glamorous or high-profile role.

To create a highly functioning team, athletes must buy into their assigned roles. Coaches should keep this in mind when selecting their teams. Some players, no matter how talented, will never fit into a team concept. When finalizing his roster for the 1980 Winter Olympics, "Miracle on Ice" architect Herb Brooks emphasized he didn't necessarily want the most talented players, he wanted the right ones.

Besides having the right players, you must handle them the right way. Any coach who puts one athlete ahead of another is looking for trouble in the locker room. If there is one set of rules for the stars and one for the rest, the team will likely splinter.

To fully appreciate what's involved in building a team, learn about psychologist Bruce Tuckman. He described four stages of team formation:

- **Forming** (getting to know each other)
- **Storming** (confronting issues)
- **Norming** (deciding on work habits)
- **Performing** (functioning as a unit)

Tuckman's work shows clearly how the players create their own team. It's important though, that coaches help them with this process. As Coach Pritchard emphasizes, the coach's job is to create an environment and monitor progress. Experienced coaches know each team has a unique cast of characters, and team unity can't be forced. It has to develop from within.

Players can learn very specific things from team-building exercises both big and small:

- **Trust.** In order to be a good teammate, a player must not only trust, but be trustworthy. After all, teammates can trust me with all their heart, but if I am not worthy of that trust, everything will break down. Players must forgive good-faith mistakes and weaknesses in others, and be forgiven in turn. The key phrase is "good faith." If a player has put full effort into practice and made a crucial mistake in a game, forgiveness should be forthcoming. But when lazy habits lead to mistakes that hurt the whole team, the issue must be brought up. That leads us to:

- **Communication.** Everything can't be rosy over the course of the season. Some issues need to be talked about, and when this happens, players must feel free to do it. Keep in mind that communication can be verbal or otherwise. Rolling eyes convey contempt. Body language can say more than words ever could. Listening is a huge part of communication; when your athletes speak, will they be heard?
- **Respect.** Any time you put more than one human being in a room or on a field, you will have various differences: values, attitudes, cultures and customs. Working with, and succeeding with, these various differences can bring immense satisfaction. But it requires a commitment by all to make it work.
- **Common goal.** Strange as it sounds, not everyone on the team has the same goal. As coach, you would hope that everyone wanted team success, but again, there are vast differences in people. Some crave attention and recognition; others pursue their own stats. Some are in it just for fun, others for the social aspect. Getting everyone focused on a common goal can test the powers of any coach.
- **Problem-solving.** All of athletics is problem-solving. If you're playing in goal against world-class striker Christiano Ronaldo, you've got a problem. Any time the other team has more speed, strength or skill than your team, you have a problem that must be solved. Your collective willingness to confront and go to work on the problem is an important part of your team identity.
- **Dealing with adversity.** No season will ever go smoothly. Something will always happen. There will be injuries, arguments, unexpected losses and slumps. What will happen to the team when these things arise? What will the team's attitude be in the face of bad circumstances?

Adversity can either ruin you or make you great. Response is all in the team attitude.

- **Selflessness.** To be fully vested teammates, players must give up a part of themselves, both on the field and off. They must act like they are part of something bigger than themselves. Their actions affect all. You've no doubt heard about big-time athletes who got into trouble the night before a big game. Their actions destroyed the dreams of teammates who had worked very hard for that moment.

- **Individual recognition.** Make sure that everyone on the team is recognized for some contribution. Help your players to see and aspire to the qualities of teammates. Some players bring physical gifts. Others bring humor, perspective, fitness, tenacity, intelligence. If everyone feels that they have something definite and specific to contribute, and everybody knows about these attributes, you are on your way to having an effective and cohesive unit. Teammates who recognize and help each other are connected to the team's success. You can either build barriers or bridges.

Coach, if you want an improved record and a more highly functioning team, remember to keep your finger on the pulse of your team, pay attention to the little things, and keep team-building an important part of your program.

Notes:

How much attention do you give team-building in your program?

What can you use from this chapter to build a better team and improve team performance?

What can you do starting this season?

Will you do it?

CHAPTER TEN

The Journey Never Ends

"If I have seen further than others, it is by standing upon the shoulders of giants."

ISAAC NEWTON
English physicist

"Far and away the best prize that life has to offer is the chance to work hard at work worth doing."

THEODORE ROOSEVELT
26th President of the United States

Cosmic philosopher Dr. Carl Sagan once said that the Hubble Telescope is more than just a tool for discovery. It is an object whose very existence gives insight into the soul of humanity. Sagan said that centuries from now when man has passed from the Earth, visitors will come and see the telescope pointed out toward the cosmos, not in toward ourselves, and they will know that we were a curious people.

"Understanding is a kind of ecstasy," said Sagan, a passionately curious observer of the heavens.

Great coaches know what Sagan meant. They pursue knowledge with the same passion as the legendary scientists. They learn, they teach, they meet colleagues who share their interest, and all the while, they are doing something they love. Their curiosity and passion fill their lives with meaning. Great coaches are always learning, evolving, discovering.

You began your journey the first time you watched a great player, picked up a ball or kicked one. At that moment, you began your 10,000 hours, those 10,000 hours that researchers have shown are necessary for mastery in any given area.

At some point, your focus changed from running, kicking, throwing, catching or jumping. Suddenly you wanted to help others do these things. This effort is no less mystifying than the universe: You are trying to teach skill, tactics, fitness and mental skills, and do this all while providing motivation and a fun environment.

No matter what you have learned or achieved, this journey

must continue. Great coaches keep growing. Pat Summitt tells of flying to Chicago to learn more about a single aspect of the game. John Wooden used to identify one area of improvement, and dedicate his off-season to it. It's fun to think about what the speakers at these clinics must have thought, having a Summitt or a Wooden in the audience taking notes!

Here are some things to keep in mind as you make your journey of discovery:

- **Great insights are available to everyone.** Coach Pritchard says, "Everyone who got where they are started where they were." Remember Bill James, revolutionizing baseball statistics while he worked in a pork and beans factory?

- **Great coaches understand that the only thing they can absolutely count on is change.** The moment you are not satisfied with what you see, you have the seeds for change and a chance for a great discovery. Perhaps it will be better training, motivation, or practice techniques. A case in point: Piggy Lambert, the man who coached John Wooden, valued speed more than height. He wound up inventing the fast break.

  Just like your athletes, you will go through phases, levels and plateaus. At one point, your fascination might be with drills; at another point it could be with tactics or fitness. Then you might get to the level of Anson Dorrance of the University of North Carolina women's soccer program, who says that at a certain point it is not about the drills, it's about finding ways to motivate and challenge players. Or you may find some kinship with Los Angeles Lakers Coach Phil Jackson, who sees a spiritual aspect to coaching.

- **Great coaches learn how to learn.** If you read every coaching article, watch every DVD and attend every clinic, you are bound to hear lots of information, some of it contradictory. Novices may soak up everything, but experienced coaches can look at information and see what will fit in.

In this book, we mention the work of coaches from a variety of sports. Make yourself a student of them, no matter what their field. You can always pick up a quote, a practice planning tip, or a motivational story. As much as you read books, learn to read players even more. See how they absorb information. Are they visual, auditory or kinesthetic learners? Discover different techniques for motivating different types of players: Some are motivated simply through belonging, others through challenges, some through recognition, and more through healthy competition. A coach who is a student of the game may go to a clinic hoping to find just one nugget of information to help accomplish this.

On rare occasions, you may even hear something so exciting that you're prepared to throw away a lot of what you do. In cases like this, make sure the new information is grounded in sound principles and aligned with your values and philosophy and is not another "flavor of the month."

- **Be focused on the right thing at the right time.** There is so much to understand about coaching. Besides skill, tactics and conditioning, there is scouting, teaching, mental conditioning, team-building and dynamics, game management, motivation, dealing with parents and practice planning. Unlike the student who underlines everything with red marker, good coaches are selective about what to emphasize. They know that if everything is important, then nothing is important. Be focused on what your players need most right now, and dig into learning about it.
- **Keep raising the bar.** Never "finally arrive" as a coach. Never become an expert, at least in your own mind. Hall of Fame baseball manager Earl Weaver once wrote a book

called *It's What You Learn After You Know It All That Counts*. Bruce Springsteen put it another way in one of his lyrics: "You gotta stay hungry." Hunger and humility. Be on guard against too much certainty. Mark Twain said, "It ain't so much the things we don't know that get us into trouble. It's the things we know that just ain't so."

- **Work with and hire people who are not like you.** We all have strengths, weaknesses and faults. Your people should have a variety of personalities and different skill sets to better serve your players and program. See the good in those who challenge you a bit and don't see things exactly as you do. Through working with others, you will grow. Others can help raise your attitude, work ethic, energy level and willingness to take risks. Encourage your people not to be afraid to cross the line of what is safe. As coaches we can't expect our athletes to be brave warriors and risk-takers if we always take the safe or risk-free approach. How do you suppose your players or staff would grade you on this?

- **Look past productivity and results. It's about relationships.** As you go through your coaching career, you will think more and more of the people with whom you have been in contact. And you will realize more and more that the journey is really about those people. As this is being written, players from a prominent national basketball program were just arrested and charged with drug and weapons offenses. How much were their high school and college coaches committed to developing the whole person? As your coaching journey moves forward, be sure to grow as a teacher of life skills. What effect have you had upon your players and staff? What could you do to make the experience more valuable for them?

- **Have the relationship of a mentor as well as a coach.** One of the biggest compliments any coach can receive is to have a player go on to become a coach. It means the coach has sown passion in someone's soul. As quoted earlier, as a coach you have a choice of between being "the sage on the stage" or "a guide on the side." Be a guide on the side and empower those around you to greatness. It's all about others.

- **Remember to give back.** At a certain point in your development, you might become just as interested in writing an article as in reading one. You might have just as much fun giving a clinic as you would in attending one. There's a saying that people teach what they most need to learn. Everything you teach can make you a better coach. You will never know something as well as you will after you have taught it to someone else.

- **Have patience and forgiveness.** You have it with your athletes. You have to show it with yourself. Becoming a great coach takes time. It is difficult. In looking back on his career in volleyball, Coach Tully realizes that nearly everything he learned for the first 10 years turned out to be wrong. It's tempting to regret all that lost time, but without those mistakes, the subsequent insights would never have been so joyful. The biggest realization is that all your coaching endeavors ultimately involve people. When a player makes a mistake, it may go in the record book, and it perhaps loses a game. But when a coach makes a mistake, it can diminish the self-esteem of a young person. That's why coaches — even as they strive — must forgive themselves, as well as others. Never stop learning, communicating, teaching and caring.

- **Grow to respect differences.** Understand that certain players may simply have different beliefs and value systems than you do. Through experience and wisdom, begin to be a bit more flexible and tolerant and not cram your beliefs down their throats. Reach and inspire your players by becoming a story-teller. Stories are a great teaching vehicle. Have a vision for each player. Help them see and reach the level where you already see them.

- **Keep hanging around good coaches.** It's contagious. We become what we think about and do most of the time. Read biographies of great figures. Pay particular attention to the standards they set for themselves, and keep holding yourself to a similar standard. Make sure you are holding to your philosophy and personal goals in all that you do and say. Avoid second-guessing.

If this all seems like a lot of hard work, it is. Even with all the passion you have, you can still get burned out. Make time to recharge your batteries and rebuild your enthusiasm. Remember, it's all about the energy you bring to your team. Continue to work at the balance between coaching and your personal life. Don't be one of those coaches who sleeps in the office. Smell the roses. Balance can make you a better coach and better person.

Love and respect your game. Give back to your game.

Notes:

Is there a past mistake for which you should forgive yourself?

What is your attitude toward mistakes? Do you see them as fatal flaws or learning experiences?

Do you see a connection between how you view your own mistakes and how you see those of your players?

What can you do to change?

Thanks for taking your valuable time to read this.
We wish you continued success in sports and life.

All the best,
Gary Pritchard and Mike Tully